VEGETARIAN DISHES
from
MY KOREAN HOME

FLAVORFUL KOREAN RECIPES IN SIMPLE STEPS

SHIN KIM 김신정

www.banchanstory.com

ISBN 978-0-9982249-0-9

Artistic and cultural direction by Shin Kim and Shinhee Kim
Book design by Tara Mayberry, TeaBerry Creative
Recipes edited by Deri Reed
Author portrait photography by Jamahl Richardson

Printed in the United States of America
10 9 8 7 6 5 4 3 2 1
First Edition

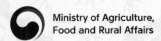
Ministry of Agriculture, Food and Rural Affairs

KFF 한식재단
KOREAN FOOD FOUNDATION

THE TASTE OF KOREA
HANSIK

CONTENTS

INTRODUCTION

In the past few years the popularity of Korean food has surged to new heights in the U.S. People are enjoying grilled pork and kimchi in smoky BBQ restaurants, downing soju shots over hearty stews, and discovering modern interpretations of Korean cuisine by young chefs, right here in New York and other major cities. I feel lucky to live in this moment when people are taking an interest in Korean food and want to learn more about Korea's culinary culture and tradition.

Yet, we have only begun to scratch the surface of this wondrous cuisine. Korea is a country of harsh winters and humid summers, with three sides exposed to the sea and 70 percent of the land mountainous and not suitable for farming. Koreans take pride in the variety and quality of seafood—fish and sea vegetables—and make use of them in multiple ways. Herbs and vegetables from nearby hills and mountains are eaten fresh, dried, dried and rehydrated, and fermented throughout the year. In addition to rice, a variety of grains and legumes are a part of Koreans' everyday diet.

After Buddhism had seen its glory as a national religion for 1,000 years, then survived through 500 years of religious oppression, its practice of vegan cooking and eating as a part of meditation is welcomed even by non-Buddhists. Since the Korean War in the 1950s, much of the communal, agrarian society has been transformed into a service-oriented, industrialized country. With one-fifth of the 50 million people living in the crowded capital city of Seoul, the communal tradition of making huge batches of kimchi with neighbors in late fall now remains more as a ceremonial activity. The latest hit TV show of quick-cooking meals in easy steps with simple ingredients is a glimpse into how so many Koreans now lead lives so busy that they are left with not enough time or space to cook at home. It is a cuisine that continues to evolve, constantly moving to balance the fading tradition and the latest trend, with practical reality in mind.

All of these factors are reflected in Korean cuisine as it is today, a cuisine that spans much wider and deeper than charred BBQ and fiery kimchi. (But I *do* include vegan kimchi recipes in the book.) Here, I attempt to introduce another part of Korean cuisine through 30 flavorful vegetarian dishes that make up an important part of Korean home cooking. We will delve into how fresh, seasonal ingredients meet with a handful of fermented, aged sauces and together they create a whole spectrum of flavors from deeply hearty to refreshingly piquant. The recipes are a collection of everyday dishes I grew up with in Korea and have taught in cooking classes in New York, recipes I have learned from my teachers, and even the dishes I adapted from watching the latest cooking shows in Korea. All of the recipes are updated for home cooks in the U.S., so you can cook Korean dishes with a few essential Korean ingredients and locally available vegetables. You will also be able to mix and match different sauces and ingredients from these recipes, creating your own Korean food just like Koreans do. I hope this book serves as an introduction to Korean home cooking, and also as a base to help expand your culinary creativity beyond the simple, healthy vegetarian recipes here.

Autumn, 2016—Shin

HOW TO USE THIS COOKBOOK

This cookbook includes 30 simple, healthy Korean vegetarian recipes used in Korean home cooking. It can be thought of as a guide for exploring Korean home cooking that proudly features vegetables at the center. Here are some helpful notes about the ingredients and instructions that appear throughout the book.

I have marked common dietary concerns in the table of contents and at each recipe. Note that some recipes that are marked as gluten-free, nut-free, vegan, or spicy can include optional ingredients that would make the dish not gluten-free, nut-free, vegan, or spicy. On the other hand, for recipes that I have not marked vegan or gluten-free, you can usually eliminate the eggs, substitute honey with other sweeteners, or use gluten-free soy sauce to make them vegan or gluten-free.

 GLUTEN-FREE   NUT-FREE   VEGAN    SPICY

I recommend that you follow the recipes exactly at least once to get a better understanding of how each dish is supposed to be made and to taste. As you cook through the recipes, make note of the ratios of the main ingredients to the seasoning/sauce/dressing mix, collectively called "yangnyeom" in Korea, and listed separately in the ingredient section. You may even recognize many of the familiar Korean flavors from these yangnyeom mixes, which set the tone and flavor for the main ingredients and for the whole dish.

Once you feel comfortable with different sets of yangnyeom, experiment by mixing and matching a sauce from one recipe with vegetables from another and add your own flare. For example, the spicy gochujang sauce used for Spicy Rice Cake Stew (page 46) is a delicious alternative to the soy-sesame sauce in the tofu and mushroom dish (page 20).

Opposite is a cheatsheet of sorts for some of the basic seasoning bases that are used in the recipes that you can use for easy reference.

Basic Ratios of Select Korean Seasoning Bases (양념 Yangnyeom)
In addition to the main ingredients in the sauce, one or more aromatic ingredients such as garlic, scallion, sesame seeds, and sesame oil are added to the seasoning base in order to bolster the flavor.

PAGE	YANGNYEOM BASE	RATIO BY VOLUME	GOOD FOR...
6	Kimchi Dressing	2 parts rice vinegar 1 part red pepper flakes 1 part sweetener	Salad (radish, cucumber)
14	Soy Paste Dip (Ssamjang)	2 parts soybean paste 1 part red pepper paste	Crudités, bibimbap sauce
20	Soy-Sesame Sauce (Bulgogi Sauce)	2 parts soy sauce 1 part sesame oil 1 part sweetener	Braised tofu and mushrooms
22	Sweet Soy Syrup	3 parts rice syrup or other syrup 2 parts soy sauce	Braised root vegetable (burdock, lotus)
30	Spicy Sesame Dressing	1 part red pepper flakes 1 part sesame oil 1 part soy sauce	Shishito peppers, noodle soup, bibimbap
46	Spicy Gochujang Sauce	1 part red pepper paste 1 part red pepper flakes 1 part soy sauce	Braise, stews
56	Spicy Tangy Gochujang Sauce (Gochujang Vinaigrette)	1 part red pepper paste 1 part rice vinegar	Noodle salad, seaweed salad, spicy dip

Notes on Key Korean Ingredients Used in This Book

Below are explanations on the major ingredients used in the recipes that are also essential in Korean cooking in general.

KOREAN RED PEPPER PASTE (고추장 gochujang), KOREAN SOYBEAN PASTE (된장 doenjang), and KOREAN SOY SAUCE (간장 ganjang) are the foundational trinity of fermented sauces that make up a major part of Korean flavors. Sometimes they are used on their own and featured as a prominent ingredient in a dish; other times they are mixed together in different ratios along with other ingredients to create varied degrees of refined heat and luscious pungency. Sometimes, you won't even notice they are in a dish, but you might notice an undertone of oomph. You can easily find them in Korean and Asian markets. Look for high-quality, artisanal brands as they do have a much deeper, cleaner flavor.

KOREAN SOUP SOY SAUCE (국간장 guk ganjang) is also called HOUSE SOY SAUCE (집간장 jip ganjang) in Korea. Traditionally, soup soy sauce, made with only soybeans, salt, and water, has a saltier and deeper flavor than regular soy sauce, which may have other flavoring additives. I list the soup soy sauce in the recipe when it is better to use it, but feel free to use gluten-free soy sauce or regular soy sauce if you have difficulty finding the traditional Korean soup soy sauce.

KOREAN RED PEPPER FLAKES (고춧가루 gochu garu) are used in making kimchi as well as many Korean dishes for a forward spicy heat, as opposed to the red pepper paste for a more rounded, sweeter heat. It has a medium level of spicy heat with fruity fragrance.

DRIED SHIITAKE MUSHROOMS (표고버섯 pyogo beoseot) are especially important in vegetarian Korean cooking. They are packed with concentrated savory flavor that is released when the mushrooms are rehydrated before being used in cooking. The soaking water itself is also used to enhance the savory depth in a short time.

DRIED KELP (다시마 dashima) is another important savory ingredient in vegetarian Korean cooking. Like dried shiitake mushrooms, dried kelp is soaked to be bloomed before using. It has a subtle, briny flavor that deepens a savory note in soups and stews.

NEUTRAL VEGETABLE OILS, such as vegetable oil, canola oil, or sunflower seed oil, are used as they allow high-heat cooking without imparting their own flavor to the dish. Since there are no olives or coconuts grown in Korea, it is best to avoid olive oil or coconut oil in traditional Korean cooking.

DARK-COLORED TOASTED SESAME OIL is another prominent ingredient in Korean cooking. It is often mixed with neutral vegetable oil and used in cooking, but to get the most out of this nutty, aromatic oil, use it sparingly as a finishing oil at the end right before serving.

COARSE SEA SALT is used mainly for the initial step of treating vegetables to help release the vegetable liquid. Because of its big crystals, coarse sea salt is not absorbed into the vegetable quickly and is washed away before the next step. Both Korean coarse sea salt and American coarse sea salt can do the job. I'd recommend that you experiment and make note of how salty vegetables become, and how quickly, when you use a particular brand.

KOSHER SALT is used for cooking in this book for accessibility and consistency.

Kimchi and Pickles

Kimchi—the comprehensive term covers all fermented vegetables—is a national staple dish of Korea. Along with a simple, vegan version of the most well-known spicy napa cabbage kimchi, you will find recipes for a non-spicy radish kimchi and a quick cucumber salad with kimchi dressing that requires no fermentation. Popular Korean pickles that complement so many dishes are also included in this section.

SIMPLE VEGAN NAPA CABBAGE KIMCHI
(막김치 Mahk Kimchi)

Of the 200-plus kimchi variations on record, spicy napa cabbage kimchi, seasoned with lots of red pepper flakes, garlic, ginger, and fish sauce, is the most well known. My version is both vegan and gluten-free as I don't include fish sauce and use traditional Korean soup soy sauce, which is naturally gluten-free. Banana, although not a common ingredient in traditional kimchi, works well as a binder for the paste as well as a natural sweetener, and danhobak, a.k.a. kabocha, keeps the kimchi color bright. The banana flavor will dissipate as the kimchi starts to ferment. Make this small batch of kimchi and enjoy it as is, or use in Kimchi Fried Rice (page 58) or Simple Kimchi Stew (page 44) as it continues to ferment and develop its pungently pleasant flavors over time.

Makes about 1½ quarts / 2 kg

1 (3-pound / 1.4-kg) head napa cabbage

½ cup / 100 g coarse sea salt

SIMPLE VEGAN KIMCHI PASTE

1 kabocha squash (단호박 danhobak)

1 medium yellow onion, cut into chunks

1 medium ripe banana, peeled and cut into chunks

¼ cup / 60 ml Korean soup soy sauce (국간장 guk ganjang) or gluten-free soy sauce

8 to 10 garlic cloves, peeled

1 (1-inch / 2.5-cm) piece ginger, peeled

1 to 2 tablespoons sugar

½ cup / 40 g Korean red pepper flakes, coarse ground for kimchi

1. Cut the cabbage in half lengthwise, then in half lengthwise again. Cut out the core and discard. Cut the cabbage into 1-inch / 2.5-cm pieces and place in a large bowl. Add the salt and toss the cabbage to mix. Let rest at room temperature until the cabbage is mostly wilted, 1 to 2 hours, tossing occasionally for even salting all around.

2. To make the kimchi paste: Cook the whole kabocha until soft, either in the microwave for 5 to 7 minutes or in boiling water in a medium pot for about 20 minutes. Drain and let it cool to room temperature. Cut in half, scoop out the seeds, and scoop out the flesh. Discard the seeds and reserve ¼ cup / 60 g of the flesh. Freeze the remaining flesh for another dish.

3. In a blender, combine the kabocha, onion, banana, soy sauce, garlic, ginger, and 1 tablespoon sugar and blend to a smooth consistency. Transfer the paste to a medium bowl and stir in the red pepper flakes until completely combined. Taste and adjust seasoning. It should taste like the kimchi you want to eat—spicy, salty, sweet, and flavorful all around. Mix in the remaining 1 tablespoon sugar, if desired. Set aside.

4. When most of the cabbage pieces are wilted, wash the cabbage in cold water 2 or 3 times to get rid of salt on the outer layer. Gently squeeze out excess water and place the washed cabbage in a large, clean bowl.

5. Mix the seasoning paste into the cabbage. Cover with plastic wrap and let it rest at room temperature, away from the direct sunlight, for 1 to 2 days, until bubbles start forming on the surface. Taste to check if it is developing a tangy flavor. Store in an airtight container in the refrigerator for up to 1 month. Flavor will continue to develop throughout its storage period.

VEGETARIAN DISHES FROM MY KOREAN HOME

WHITE RADISH KIMCHI

(동치미 Dongchimi)

Water-based kimchi is especially popular in winter as a side dish as well as a broth base for chilled noodle soup. Fall fruits are added for natural sweetness, but you can add more sugar if you are short of fruit. For my children's cooking classes, I cut the radish into bite-size cubes and add red and yellow bell peppers. The kids help by cutting the bell peppers into squares, triangles, or flower shapes using small cookie cutters. It is a fun, colorful, and not-spicy way to introduce kimchi to kids.

Makes about 2 quarts / 2 liters

4 cups / 1 liter filtered water

4 tablespoons / 50 g coarse sea salt

1 to 2 tablespoons sugar

1 (2-pound / 900-g) Korean radish (무 mu) or daikon radish, cut into 2-inch / 5-cm sticks

½ medium onion, sliced

½ medium Asian pear, a.k.a. apple pear (배 bae), cored and thinly sliced

½ medium sweet apple, such as Gala or Fuji, cored and thinly sliced

2 scallions, cut into 2-inch / 5-cm lengths

8 garlic cloves, peeled and sliced

1 (1-inch / 2.5-cm) piece ginger, peeled and sliced

1 Korean red chile pepper or red Fresno chile pepper, thinly sliced with seeds (optional, for spicy heat)

1. Bring the water to a boil over high heat. Add 2 tablespoons of the salt and 1 tablespoon of the sugar and dissolve completely. (Use 2 tablespoons of sugar if the fruits are not sweet or not available.) Let cool to room temperature.

2. Toss the radish sticks in the remaining 2 tablespoons salt. Let rest until the outer layer of the radish sticks have softened slightly and the liquid is released, about 20 minutes. Wash off any remaining salt from the radish in cold water until there is no slimy feel to the touch. Drain and gently squeeze out excess water.

3. Combine the onion, pear, apple, scallions, garlic, ginger, and red pepper, if using, in a 3-quart container with a lid. Place the radish on top of the bed of vegetables and pour the salt water from step 1 over the radish. Place a piece of parchment paper to touch the surface and press it down with a small bowl so that the vegetables are kept immersed in the liquid and not exposed to air.

4. Cover the container with a lid or plastic wrap. Let sit at room temperature to ferment for 1 to 3 days. Check every day to see that bubbles start appearing on the surface and the liquid has developed a sweet, tangy flavor.

5. Remove and discard the parchment paper and apple and pear pieces. Store the kimchi in the refrigerator for up to 1 month.

KIMCHI-STYLE SPICY TANGY CUCUMBER SALAD

(오이생채 Oi Saengchae)

Drawing out excess liquid from a vegetable by tossing it in coarse sea salt is a common first step in prepping vegetables in Korean cooking, including making kimchi; it helps the vegetable remain crunchy for a longer period of time. This salad is similar to spicy, tangy, sweet kimchi but with a bright, refreshing note and minus the wait for fermentation. Serve it cold as a traditional Korean side dish with rice. You can also use it as a topping for cold noodle salad, or a fixing for tacos and burgers. I love the cucumber version in the summer, but also try it with red radish or carrot. I like using Korean radish (무 mu) instead of cucumber in the wintertime.

Makes 4 side servings

6 to 7 Persian cucumbers
(a.k.a. mini cucumbers),
cut into thin rounds

2 tablespoons coarse sea salt

QUICK KIMCHI DRESSING

2 tablespoons rice vinegar

1 tablespoon Korean red pepper flakes

1 tablespoon sugar

1 scallion, finely chopped

1 garlic clove, minced or grated

1 teaspoon toasted sesame seeds

1. Toss the cucumbers with the salt in a large bowl. Let them rest just until the cucumbers start to soften and sweat, 5 to 10 minutes.

2. To make the kimchi dressing: Mix all the ingredients in a small bowl.

3. Rinse the cucumbers with cold water to wash off the salt. Squeeze gently to remove excess water.

4. Mix the cucumbers with the dressing and refrigerate for about 30 minutes before serving.

PICKLED YELLOW RADISH

(단무지 Danmuji)

The origin of this condiment is Japanese pickled radish (takuan), but it is also a condiment for many Korean dishes, like Spicy Rice Cake Stew (page 46). You can purchase danmuji in packages in Asian markets, but it is very easy to make at home. Include the turmeric powder if you like the distinctively bright yellow color in your pickle, or omit it to keep the pickle naturally white. Once you have the basic recipe down, you can easily make variations (below) for numerous applications for other Korean dishes.

Makes about 1 quart / 1 liter

1 (1-pound / 450-g) small daikon radish or Korean radish (무 mu)

¾ cup / 180 ml rice vinegar

¾ cup / 180 ml water

¼ cup / 40 g sugar

½ teaspoon kosher salt

1 teaspoon turmeric powder (optional)

1 teaspoon black peppercorns (optional)

4 garlic cloves, sliced (optional)

1. Peel and cut the radish in half lengthwise, then into ¼-inch / 0.5-cm slices. Place in a medium bowl.

2. In a medium saucepan, mix together the rice vinegar, water, sugar, and salt, along with the turmeric, peppercorns, and/or garlic, if using. Bring to a boil, then pour over the radish. Let cool to room temperature.

3. Place the danmuji and the pickling liquid in an airtight container and store in the refrigerator, where it will keep for up to 1 month. Its color and flavor will continue to develop over the next couple of days.

VARIATIONS

* *Different cuts for different dishes—Cut the radish into strips for gimbap (rice rolls wrapped in seaweed), or cut it into very thin slices and use the radish sheet as a vegetable wrap along with leafy green vegetables. You can also dice the radish and omit the turmeric to keep the color white and serve as a condiment for Korean fried chicken.*
* *Red danmuji—Add a few slices of a red beet to infuse red color to make this pickled radish pretty in any shape!*

SPICY PEPPER PICKLES

(고추장아찌 Gochu Jangajji)

Gochu jangajji is a versatile Korean condiment that complements just about everything as a side dish. Serve the drained pickles as a stand-alone side dish or with their liquid with savory pancakes, such as the Scallion Pancakes (page 16) and Crispy Squash Pancakes (page 18) instead of a dipping sauce. The soy sauce base, once steeped with aromatic vegetables and spicy peppers, can also be used to replace some of the regular soy sauce used in other dishes, serving as your own flavor building block. Jalapeño peppers are easily accessible in the U.S. and have a similar heat level as Korean peppers, so I often use them in my Korean cooking. I also mix spicy peppers with non-spicy ones to balance the heat level. Once you have soy sauce, rice vinegar, and peppers that make up the main flavor base, feel free to rely on seasonings and aromatics from the fridge to add savory or sweet flavors to the pickle. If you prefer a deeper soy sauce flavor, use only ¼ cup rice vinegar; if you'd like a balanced flavor of salty and tangy, use the ½ cup or more.

Makes about 1 quart / 1 liter

½ pound / 230 g Korean green chile peppers or jalapeño peppers

½ pound / 230 g long green peppers or any pepper with little or no heat

2 Korean red chile peppers (optional)

SOY SAUCE BASE

2 cups / 480 ml soy sauce

¼ to ½ cup / 60 to 120 ml rice vinegar

½ medium onion, thinly sliced

5 garlic cloves, sliced

1 (1-inch / 2.5-cm) piece ginger, peeled and sliced

1 dried shiitake mushroom (표고버섯 pyogo beoseot)

1 (2-inch / 5-cm) piece dried kelp (다시마 dashima)

1 teaspoon whole black peppercorns

1. Wear plastic gloves and cut all the peppers into thin slices. Put the peppers in a large bowl, including the seeds.

2. To make the soy sauce base: Combine the soy sauce, rice vinegar, onion, garlic, ginger, shiitake, kelp, and peppercorns in a medium saucepan and bring to a boil over high heat.

3. Pour the soy sauce mixture over the peppers and let them cool to room temperature. The liquid level will rise slightly as it cools.

4. Store the peppers and the liquid in an airtight container in the refrigerator for up to 1 month. It is best to let the pickles rest overnight before tasting. The flavor will continue to develop for the next few days.

CHUNJINAM

I had the good fortune of living with the Buddhist nun Jeong Kwan in the Chunjinam hermitage in the spring of 2016. Although I was there for only ten days, I was able to participate in the temple life. Away from the bustling city, I learned about seasonal herbs and vegetables, and fermentation and other slow preservation processes. Simply put, it was an eye-opening experience.

Banchan, More Than Side Dishes

Banchan is a comprehensive term for the dishes that accompany rice or noodles. It ranges from simple preparations on small plates to substantial main dishes. The most popular Korean dishes as well as lesser-known home favorites are presented here so you can try a wide range of banchan.

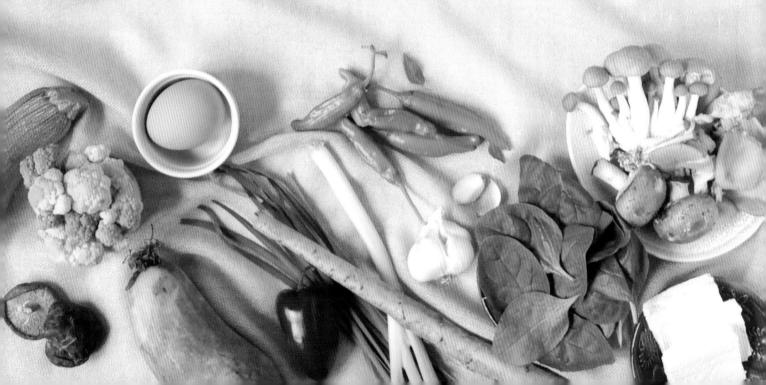

SOY PASTE DIP

Korean flavors from its foundational sauces (page vii)—doenjang and gochujang—are very forward in this dip and will leave a flavorful, strong, and pungent imprint. Ssamjang is usually served as a dip with raw vegetable crudités, and a small dollop of it is a must-have for a lettuce wrap with barbecued meat. And its many variations add extra oomph to different Korean dishes. Try mixing it into bibimbap; you will find it less spicy, yet still flavorful compared with your usual bibimbap sauce. I like to include the optional chopped walnuts for the nutty, crunchy bite.

Makes 1 cup

½ cup / 140 g Korean fermented soybean paste (된장 doenjang)

¼ cup / 60 g Korean fermented red pepper paste (고추장 gochujang)

¼ cup / 30 g walnuts, toasted and finely chopped (optional)

3 garlic cloves, minced or grated

2 scallions, finely chopped

2 tablespoons toasted sesame oil

1 tablespoon sugar

2 teaspoons toasted sesame seeds

1 to 2 tablespoons honey, to taste

1. Mix together all the ingredients.

2. Adjust consistency and sweetness with honey.

SCALLION PANCAKES

(파전 Pajeon)

Koreans make savory pancakes with just about every vegetable out there, with scallion pancakes being the most famous. Prepackaged batter mix is available in Korean markets, but I like to make it from scratch and add brown rice flour for my own version. When I make vegetable pancakes, the ratio is always lots of vegetables to just enough batter to keep them together, achieving a crispy texture in doing so. This is certainly one of the most delicious ways to eat lots of scallions in one sitting! You can make the simple sauce below for dipping, or serve it with the Spicy Pepper Pickles (page 10).

Makes 4 medium pancakes, 4 side servings

PANCAKES

½ cup / 80 g all-purpose flour

½ cup / 80 g brown rice flour

1 teaspoon baking powder

½ teaspoon kosher salt

¾ cup / 180 ml water

1 large egg

2 garlic cloves, minced or grated

Pinch ground black pepper

10 to 15 scallions (about 200 g)

Neutral vegetable oil, for pan-frying

SIMPLE DIPPING SAUCE

1 tablespoon soy sauce

2 teaspoons rice vinegar

½ teaspoon toasted sesame seeds (optional)

½ teaspoon Korean red pepper flakes (optional)

1. To make the pancakes: Combine the flours, baking powder, salt, water, egg, garlic, and pepper and whisk to a consistency of smooth pancake batter.

2. Trim the scallions by removing the roots and outer layer. Cut into 2-inch / 5-cm pieces, then cut the thick, white parts in half lengthwise. Mix the scallions into the batter.

3. Heat a large skillet over medium heat and drizzle in enough oil to generously coat the bottom.

4. When the oil is shimmering, add one-fourth of the batter and spread quickly. Raise the heat to medium-high. When the edges of the pancake turn crispy golden and the middle part starts to dry, about 5 minutes, check the bottom. When it has turned golden brown, flip to the other side. Cook until the bottom is golden brown, about 5 minutes longer. Transfer to a plate and keep warm. Repeat with the remaining batter, adding oil as necessary to keep the skillet coated in oil, to make 3 pancakes.

5. To make the dipping sauce: Combine the ingredients in a small bowl.

6. Cut the pancakes into 6 or 8 wedges and serve the pancakes hot with the simple dipping sauce.

CRISPY SQUASH PANCAKES

(애호박전 Aehobak Jeon)

This adaptation from the latest hit cooking show in Korea—*Mr. Baek, the Homemade Food Master*—is another way of making vegetable pancakes. For vegetables like summer squash that have a lot of water, salting the vegetable and using its own extracted juice as a part of the batter mix helps to keep the pancakes crispy. The batter has just enough flour and a bit of starch powder as a binder to keep this mostly vegetable pancake together in the pan. Enjoy this crispy, savory squash pancake hot right out of the pan with the Scallion Pancake's dipping sauce, or with the Spicy Pepper Pickles (page 10).

Makes 2 pancakes, 2 side servings

1 medium (7-ounce / 200-g) Korean squash (애호박 aehobak), zucchini, or yellow squash

½ teaspoon kosher salt

1 garlic clove, minced or grated

Pinch ground black pepper

1 green or red Korean chile pepper or jalapeño pepper, thinly sliced (optional, for a hint of spicy heat)

¼ cup / 40 g all-purpose flour

2 tablespoons starch powder (cornstarch or potato starch)

2 tablespoons water, or more as needed

Neutral vegetable oil, for pan-frying

Simple Dipping Sauce (page 16)

1. Cut the squash into ¼-inch / 0.5-cm rounds, then cut them into sticks. Toss with the salt in a medium bowl and let rest for 15 to 20 minutes, until the squash starts to sweat and the juice is released at the bottom of the bowl.

2. Mix in the garlic, black pepper, and chile if using.

3. Add the flour, starch powder, and water and fold carefully. All of the squash strips should be coated with the wet flour mixture, which works as a binder. Add additional teaspoons of water if necessary.

4. Heat a large skillet over medium-high heat and drizzle in enough oil to coat the bottom. Add one-half of the batter and quickly spread to form a thin, even round. Cook until the edges turn crispy golden, about 5 minutes. Flip to the other side and cook until both sides are golden brown, about 5 minutes longer. Transfer to a plate and keep warm. Repeat to cook the remaining batter, adding more oil as necessary to keep the skillet hot and nicely coated with oil.

5. Serve hot with the simple dipping sauce.

BRAISED TOFU AND MUSHROOMS IN SOY-SESAME SAUCE

(두부버섯조림 Dubu Beoseot Jorim)

In Korean cooking, a sauce or dressing often sets the tone of the dish, taking on an essential role in making the main ingredients shine. This soy-sesame sauce, originally from a simple marinade for bulgogi, thinly cut grilled beef, sets the main flavor of the dish. Tofu absorbs the flavor while mushrooms of your choice boost the savory notes, making the whole dish richer.

Makes 2 servings

SOY-SESAME SAUCE

¼ cup / 60 ml water

2 tablespoons soy sauce

1 tablespoon toasted sesame oil

1 tablespoon brown sugar or raw cane sugar

2 teaspoons minced or grated garlic (2 to 3 cloves)

1 teaspoon grated ginger

TOFU AND MUSHROOMS

1 (15-ounce / 425-g) package extra-firm tofu (두부 dubu)

½ teaspoon kosher salt

Pinch ground black pepper

2 tablespoons neutral vegetable oil

2 cups / 200 g assorted mushrooms, such as oyster, beech, and button mushrooms

1 scallion, thinly sliced, for garnish

½ teaspoon toasted sesame seeds, for garnish

1. To make the soy-sesame sauce: Mix together the ingredients in a small bowl. Set aside.

2. For the tofu and mushrooms: Drain the tofu and rinse in cold water. Cut into ¼-inch / 0.5-cm square slices and place on a paper towel-lined plate. Sprinkle with ¼ teaspoon of the salt and the pepper.

3. Heat a large skillet over medium-high heat. Coat the bottom of the skillet with 1 tablespoon of the oil. Place the tofu slices, salted side down, in the skillet and sprinkle with the remaining ¼ teaspoon salt. Cook the tofu until the edges are crispy and golden, about 5 minutes. Flip to the other side and continue to cook until golden, about 5 minutes longer. Transfer the tofu to a plate.

4. Drizzle the remaining 1 tablespoon oil into the skillet and add the mushrooms. Cook over medium-high heat for a couple of minutes, until wilted.

5. Return the tofu to the pan. Reduce the heat to low and pour the soy-sesame sauce over the tofu and mushrooms. Simmer until they have absorbed most of the sauce, about 10 minutes. Remove from the heat. Sprinkle with the scallion and sesame seeds and serve warm.

VEGETARIAN DISHES FROM MY KOREAN HOME

LOTUS ROOT
IN SWEET SOY-GARLIC SYRUP

(연근조림 Yeongeun Jorim)

This side dish of lotus root in a sticky, salty, sweet syrup is a savory-sweet treat to me. With the same ingredients, it can be a quick-cooking sauté with a crunchy bite, or it can be slow-braised for over an hour with the sticky, chewy texture of the lotus root. This is a compromise of the two methods, creating the slightly crunchy and sticky texture as you bite into it and the addictive flavor from the umami-filled soy-garlic syrup, but with a shorter cooking time. (Note that the shiitake soaking water is used to cook the lotus root, which deepens its flavor. On the other hand, the lotus root is soaked in vinegar water to remove its puckering taste—so the water should be discarded afterwards.) Once you taste the sweet soy-garlic syrup, you will start recognizing the taste in other side dishes served in Korean restaurants, including black beans, burdock root, and potatoes made with the syrup as a base.

Makes 4 side servings

3 dried shiitake mushrooms (표고버섯 pyogo beoseot)

2 cups / 480 ml warm water

Vinegar

1 pound / 450 g fresh lotus root (연근 yeongeun)

SWEET SOY-GARLIC SYRUP

⅓ cup / 80 ml Korean rice syrup (조청 jocheong)

¼ cup / 60 ml soy sauce

1 tablespoon brown sugar

2 garlic cloves, minced or grated

1 (½-inch / 1.25-cm) piece ginger, peeled and grated

1 teaspoon toasted sesame seeds, for garnish

1. Soak the dried shiitake mushrooms in the warm water until soft, about 20 minutes. This can be prepared ahead by storing the mushrooms in the water in the refrigerator overnight. Cut the mushrooms into thin slices and put them back in the soaking water.

2. Fill a medium bowl with some water and a splash of vinegar. Peel the lotus root and thinly slice (about ¼ inch / 0.5 cm). Add to the vinegar-water and let soak for 10 minutes. This step will prevent oxidization and remove any puckering aftertaste in the lotus root. Drain and rinse the lotus root in fresh water.

3. In a large skillet, combine the shiitakes and their soaking water with the drained, washed lotus root slices. Bring it up to a boil, then reduce the heat and simmer until the lotus root is soft, but still with a slightly crunchy bite, about 20 minutes.

4. To make the sweet soy-garlic syrup: Mix all the ingredients together in a small bowl. Drizzle the syrup over the lotus root in the skillet and simmer, stirring occasionally, until the sauce is fully absorbed with even color, about 10 minutes.

5. Sprinkle the sesame seeds for garnish and serve warm or cold. Store leftovers in an airtight container in the refrigerator for up to 3 days.

CAULIFLOWER POPCORN IN SWEET GOCHUJANG GLAZE

(콜리플라워강정 Cauliflower Gangjeong)

This sweet, spicy gochujang glaze is present in many all-time favorites of Korean cooking, from fried chicken to grilled rice cakes. I adapted a temple-cuisine version of this dish from the Buddhist nun Dae Ahn's cookbook *Twelve Months of Temple Table* (available in Korean) by switching the main ingredient from shiitake mushrooms to cauliflower. Cauliflower has less moisture, and is therefore easier to deep-fry. If you want melt-in-your-mouth soft feel underneath the crunchy coating, try the recipe with broccoli instead.

Makes 4 side servings

SWEET GOCHUJANG GLAZE

¼ cup / 60 g Korean fermented red pepper paste (고추장 gochujang)

2 tablespoons Japanese apricot syrup (매실액 maesil aek) or agave syrup

2 tablespoons sugar

1 tablespoon soy sauce

1 tablespoon water

BATTER AND CAULIFLOWER

½ cup / 90 g potato starch

½ cup / 80 g all-purpose flour

¾ cup / 180 ml water

½ teaspoon kosher salt

Pinch ground black pepper

Neutral vegetable oil, for deep-frying

1 (1-pound / 450-g) head cauliflower, cut into bite-size florets

1 tablespoon toasted pumpkin seeds, for garnish (optional)

1. To make the gochujang glaze: In a large skillet, heat the gochujang, apricot syrup, sugar, soy sauce, and water together over low heat, stirring often to combine thoroughly. Remove from the heat when it comes to a boil. Set aside.

2. To make the batter: In a large bowl, whisk together the potato starch, flour, water, salt, and pepper to a smooth consistency.

3. Fill a deep, heavy pot about halfway with oil and heat over medium heat. Add a drop of the batter to test if the oil is hot enough for frying: The batter piece will sizzle and start floating right away when the oil is ready.

4. To fry the cauliflower: Mix the florets into the batter to coat completely. In batches, without crowding, gently shake off excess batter from the cauliflower and carefully add to the pot. The battered cauliflower will drop to the bottom first, then float to the surface as it fries. When the florets look crispy all around, about 5 minutes, transfer to a plate. Repeat with the rest of the cauliflower.

5. Before serving, fry the cauliflower one more time in batches for about 3 minutes, until the pieces have a crispy texture and golden color.

6. Transfer the cauliflower to the skillet with the gochujang glaze. Over low heat, fold gently with a wooden spoon to nicely coat the cauliflower in the glaze.

7. Transfer the glazed cauliflower to a plate and garnish with toasted pumpkin seeds, if using. Serve warm.

BURDOCK ROOT
WITH SPICY BLUEBERRY SAUCE

(우엉구이 Wooeong Gui)

When I went to the Chunjinam hermitage, one of the dishes Jeong Kwan made for us was earthy burdock root brushed with preserved mulberry sauce from the previous summer. For those of us without access to preserved mulberries, a mix of fresh blueberries and fermented pepper paste is my quick solution. It takes time to cook and pound the burdock root, which bring out its meaty texture, but that texture is a distinctive feature of this dish and it is well worth the effort.

Makes 4 side servings

SPICY BLUEBERRY SAUCE

½ cup / 85g fresh blueberries

1½ tablespoons sugar

1 tablespoon Korean fermented red pepper paste (고추장 gochujang)

1 tablespoon soy sauce

1 pound / 450 g burdock root

Splash white or rice vinegar

1 tablespoon coarse sea salt

2 tablespoons neutral vegetable oil, for pan-frying

Rice, for serving

1. To make the blueberry sauce: In a small bowl, blend together all the ingredients to a smooth consistency. Set aside.

2. Peel the burdock root with a vegetable peeler, then cut it into 2-inch / 5-cm lengths. Soak in a medium bowl of water with a splash of vinegar for 10 minutes. Drain and rinse.

3. Bring a medium saucepan of water to a boil. Add the salt and let dissolve. Add the peeled burdock root and boil over high heat until tender outside, 15 to 20 minutes. Drain and rinse with cold water.

4. Cut each burdock piece in half lengthwise. Pound with a mallet to flatten each piece to ¼ inch / 0.5 cm in thickness.

5. Heat a large skillet over medium heat and drizzle in the oil. Cook the burdock pieces in the skillet in batches until golden on the bottoms, about 5 minutes. Flip and cook until the bottoms turn golden, about 5 minutes longer.

6. Reduce the heat to low and brush the spicy blueberry sauce on the burdock root. Flip to the other side and let the sauced side caramelize slightly, only for a minute or so. Brush the top side with the sauce and flip to the other side. Let the bottom caramelize slightly, then remove from the heat.

7. Brush the top of the burdock root with the remaining sauce. Serve warm as a side dish with a bowl of rice.

VEGETARIAN DISHES FROM MY KOREAN HOME

nut free   vegan   spicy

ROLLED OMELET

(계란말이 Gyeran Mari)

The fun part of making this basic side dish of the Korean table is rolling the omelet. With a bit of patience, people in my classes have successfully made the omelet on their first try. Use a small skillet for better control and make sure to heat the skillet and drizzle enough oil to cover the bottom before adding the egg mixture. Pick colorful vegetables for the filling and chop them into small pieces so that the filling ingredients won't poke through the omelet. Relax and have fun cooking and eating!

Makes 4 side servings

6 eggs

2 teaspoons mirin
(a.k.a. Japanese cooking wine),
or 1 teaspoon sugar

½ teaspoon kosher salt

Pinch ground black pepper

¼ red bell pepper, seeded
and cut into small dice

2 tablespoons garlic chives or
2 scallions, thinly sliced

1 tablespoon neutral vegetable
oil, or more as necessary

1 sheet nori seaweed (김 gim),
cut into 4 equal squares

1. In a medium bowl, whisk the eggs, mirin, salt, and black pepper together. Add the red pepper and garlic chives or scallions and whisk to combine.

2. Heat a small skillet over medium heat and drizzle in the oil. When the oil is shimmering, tilt the skillet to cover all around. Reduce the heat to low.

3. Pour one-third of the egg mixture into the skillet and quickly tilt the skillet to spread the egg evenly. Place a piece of the seaweed in the middle of the omelet. When the egg is half-cooked, about 2 minutes, roll up the omelet from one side, using two spoons. Keep rolling until just a small flap is left. Carefully move the omelet to the other side of the skillet.

4. Add half of the remaining egg mixture and top with a piece of seaweed. Let cook for another minute, then repeat the rolling procedure, starting with the flap of the rolled egg mixture at the side of the pan. Repeat one more time with the remaining egg mixture and seaweed. Reserve the last piece of seaweed for another use. Leave the rolled omelet in the skillet for another 3 minutes over low heat, until it is cooked through.

5. Transfer the rolled omelet to a paper towel–lined plate and let it cool for 10 minutes. Cut across into ½-inch-thick / 1-cm-thick slices with a serrated knife to show the rolled insides. Serve warm or cold.

VEGETARIAN DISHES FROM MY KOREAN HOME

STEAMED SHISHITO PEPPERS WITH SESAME DRESSING

(꽈리고추찜 Ggwari Gochu Jjim)

Even with the recent popularity of blistered shishito peppers in New York restaurants, my mom's version of steamed peppers remains my favorite, and not just because it brings back memories from my childhood. The thin flour coating helps the dressing stick to the peppers and gives a nice, sticky contrast to the still slightly crunchy peppers. Although most shishito peppers are mild, you may get hit with a random, fiery spicy pepper once in a while regardless of how you cook them.

Makes 4 side servings

SPICY SESAME DRESSING

1 tablespoon soy sauce

1 tablespoon toasted sesame oil

1 tablespoon Korean red pepper flakes

2 teaspoons toasted sesame seeds

1 scallion, finely chopped

1 garlic clove, minced or grated

1 pound / 450 g shishito peppers (꽈리고추 ggwari gochu)

2 tablespoons sweet rice flour (a.k.a. glutinous rice flour; Mochiko or Bob's Red Mill brand) or all-purpose flour

Rice, for serving

1. To make the sesame dressing: Mix the ingredients together in a small bowl and set aside.

2. Snap off the tops of the peppers and discard. Wash and drain the peppers. Poke each pepper with a fork or make a small slit with a knife so that the peppers cook quickly and the steam can be released.

3. Toss the peppers in the sweet rice flour to coat with a thin layer.

4. Set up a steamer insert in a big pot. Fill the pot with hot water, about 1 inch / 2.5 cm below the steamer insert so that the water does not touch the insert.

5. Place the peppers in the steamer, cover, and bring to a boil over high heat. Steam until the coating on the peppers looks translucent with no white rice flour spots, about 10 minutes.

6. Transfer the steamed peppers to a medium bowl with tongs. Drizzle the sesame dressing over the peppers and carefully mix in the seasoning with the tongs. Taste and adjust seasoning as necessary.

7. Serve warm or cold as a side dish with rice. Store leftovers in an airtight container in the refrigerator for up to 2 days.

SPINACH IN SESAME SEASONING

(시금치나물 Sigeumchi Namul)

"Namul" refers to minimally cooked vegetables with a light seasoning that brings out the best from the vegetable. This bright green, lightly seasoned spinach is enjoyed as a basic side dish, but it can also be added to Japchae (glass noodles with vegetables, page 54), Bibimbap (assorted vegetables on a bed of rice with a spicy sauce, page 60) and gimbap (rice rolls), to name a few.

Makes 2 side servings

SESAME SEASONING

½ teaspoon Korean soup soy sauce (국간장 guk ganjang) or regular soy sauce, plus more to taste

½ teaspoon toasted sesame oil

½ teaspoon toasted sesame seeds, crushed

1 garlic clove, minced or grated (optional)

Coarse sea salt

1 bag (6 ounces / 170 g) spinach (시금치 sigeumchi)

1. To make the sesame seasoning: Mix together the ingredients in a small bowl.

2. In a large pot, bring water to a boil over high heat. Add about 2 tablespoons salt and stir to dissolve completely. Dip the spinach in the boiling water for a few seconds, just until it wilts. Drain, rinse in cold water, and squeeze out excess water from the spinach. You should have a scant ½ cup.

3. With a glove on, mix the spinach in the sesame seasoning thoroughly with your hand. Taste and adjust seasoning as necessary by adding more soy sauce.

4. Serve warm or cold. Any leftovers can be stored in the refrigerator for a day or two.

CRUMBLED TOFU WITH CROWN DAISY

(쑥갓두부무침 Ssukgat Dubu Muchim)

Crown daisy, a.k.a. edible chrysanthemum, is a common Korean ingredient available in Korean markets and some Asian markets. A handful can lift up hearty Korean stews with its unique, but subtle, fragrance. If you can't find crown daisy, feel free to replace it with the same amount of spinach!

Makes 4 side servings

SESAME SOYBEAN DRESSING

1 teaspoon Korean fermented soybean paste (된장 doenjang)

1 teaspoon soy sauce

1 teaspoon toasted sesame oil

1 garlic clove, minced or grated

½ teaspoon toasted sesame seeds, crushed

Pinch ground black pepper

2 tablespoons coarse sea salt

7 ounces / 200 g (½ of a 14-ounce package) extra-firm tofu (두부 dubu)

1 pound / 450 g crown daisy (쑥갓 ssukgat) or spinach, trimmed

1. To make the sesame soybean dressing: Mix the ingredients together in a small bowl and set aside.

2. Bring water to a boil in a medium pot over high heat. Add the salt and stir to dissolve completely. Blanch the tofu in the boiling water for 30 seconds. Scoop out the tofu with a big ladle or a spider strainer, rinse under cold water, and press gently to squeeze out excess water. Transfer to a large bowl.

3. Bring the water up to a boil again and add the crown daisy and blanch for a few seconds, just until it wilts. Drain, rinse in cold water, and squeeze hard to draw out excess water. Cut to 1-inch / 2.5-cm lengths.

4. Slowly add the dressing to the tofu, breaking the tofu with a fork or potato masher to crumble. With a glove on, add the crown daisy and mix thoroughly with your hand. Let rest for about 30 minutes, until the dressing flavor settles into the tofu and crown daisy.

5. Serve warm or cold. Any leftovers should be stored in the refrigerator only for a day or two.

SPICY WATERMELON RIND SALAD

(수박껍질무침 Subak Ggeopjil Muchim)

Long before we started talking about reducing food waste, I learned from my mom that not only is the watermelon rind edible, but it can also be a refreshing side dish. Korean cooking often stems from making the most out of what is readily available and making the accessible ingredient last a while through various preservation methods. This humble salad is a delicious example that fits in this Korean cooking spirit and a simple way to practice "nose-to-tail" eating for fruits and vegetables. The slightly spicy, tangy, crunchy watermelon rind tastes similar to Korean radish, and a hint of sweet notes from the fruit elevates the salad. Make extra and mix the leftover rind into Bibimbap (page 60) or Spicy Noodle Salad (page 56), and you will discover a new side of watermelon as a savory ingredient.

Makes 2 side servings

4 cups / 800 g thin strips of firm white rind from a watermelon

1 tablespoon kosher salt

2 tablespoons Korean fermented red pepper paste (고추장 gochujang)

1 tablespoon rice vinegar

1 scallion, thinly sliced (optional)

1 garlic clove, minced or grated (optional)

1 teaspoon toasted sesame seeds, crushed (optional)

1. Toss the watermelon rind in the salt in a large bowl. Set aside until the rind strips start to soften and release their juice, about 15 minutes. Squeeze hard to remove as much juice as possible.

2. For the simplest salad, add the red pepper paste and rice vinegar and mix thoroughly. For a more balanced savory flavor, mix in the scallion, garlic, and toasted sesame seeds. Taste and adjust seasoning as necessary.

TONGYEONG

I fell in love with Tongyeong immediately when I visited the city 5 years ago for the first time. This small city with a quaint fishing village charm is also a great base for island hopping and exploring the seascape of the southern coast. Rewards of stunning views are well worth challenging walks and hikes in this surprisingly hilly area.

VEGETARIAN DISHES FROM MY KOREAN HOME

Stews (Jjigae) and Soups

You need to learn only a couple of cooking tips and about a few essential ingredients to start creating vegetarian versions of the most popular Korean soups and stews. You will be making deep, hearty Korean soups and stews in no time!

SPICY SOFT TOFU STEW
(순두부찌개 Sundubu Jjigae)

Sundubu jjigae is one of the most requested recipes in my cooking classes. Sundubu, the Korean extra-soft tofu, rests snuggly with squash and mushrooms in a spicy, hot broth—a comforting dish that is especially welcome in the dark, cold days of winter. The simple vegetarian stew takes only 30 minutes to put together from start to finish, but the deep savory flavor from dried kelp and shiitake mushrooms makes it taste as if it has been simmering for hours.

Makes 2 main servings

1 (2-inch / 5-cm) piece dried kelp (다시마 dashima)

2 dried shiitake mushrooms (표고버섯 pyogo beoseot)

1 cup / 240 ml warm water

½ medium (about 3½ ounces / 100 g) Korean squash (애호박 aehobak) or zucchini, cut into half-moon slices

4 button mushrooms, quartered

2 garlic cloves, minced or grated

1½ tablespoons Korean red pepper flakes

1 teaspoon soy sauce

1 (11-ounce / 310-gram) package Korean extra-soft tofu (순두부 sundubu) or 1 (12-ounce / 340-gram) package silken soft tofu, cut into 4 or 5 large chunks

1 egg (optional)

1 scallion, thinly sliced, for garnish

Sprinkle of toasted sesame seeds, for garnish

Rice, for serving

1. Soak the dried kelp and shiitake mushrooms in the warm water until tender, about 20 minutes. They can also be soaked overnight in the refrigerator.

2. Remove the shiitakes from the soaking water and squeeze out excess water. Cut into thin slices and return to the water.

3. Transfer the kelp, shiitake slices, and their soaking water to a medium saucepan. Bring to a boil over high heat. Add the squash, button mushrooms, garlic, red pepper flakes, and soy sauce and bring to a boil again. Reduce the heat to medium-low and carefully add the tofu. Simmer over medium heat until the squash is soft, about 10 minutes.

4. If using, crack the egg in the middle of the pot. Simmer the stew without stirring until the egg white turns opaque. Remove from the heat. Taste and adjust seasoning if necessary. Sprinkle the scallion and sesame seeds over the stew and serve hot with rice.

SEAFOOD VARIATION

The most popular variation of the soft tofu stew is made with shellfish. Add a few quick-cooking shellfish, such as shrimp, squid slices, or cleaned clams, after the squash becomes soft. It takes only a couple of minutes until the shellfish are cooked, making the broth rich with the sweet, briny flavor of the sea.

BASIC SOYBEAN STEW

(된장찌개 Doenjang Jjigae)

This pungent, rustic Korean stew is what I return to time after time. Although commercial brands of the soybean paste (된장 doenjang) are easy to find in Korean markets, it is worthwhile to look for artisanal brands made with only the basic ingredients of soybeans, salt, and water that are fermented for a few months to years. The soybean paste, along with a couple of other flavor-packed ingredients, deepens the hearty flavor of this vegan stew. To create variations of this basic doenjang jjigae, start with the stew base and add your own vegetable combinations. Mushroom soybean stew is a popular variation in the fall, including a variety of mushrooms such as oyster mushrooms, beech mushrooms, fresh shiitake, and enoki.

Makes 2 main servings

STEW BASE

2 cups / 480 ml water

1 (2-inch / 5-cm) piece dried kelp (다시마 dashima)

2 dried shiitake mushrooms (표고버섯 pyogo beoseot)

2 tablespoons Korean fermented soybean paste (된장 doenjang), or more if needed

2 garlic cloves, minced or grated

1 medium (7-ounce / 200-g) Korean squash (애호박 aehobak) or zucchini, cut into half-moon slices

½ medium onion, cut into medium dice

4 button mushrooms, quartered

7 ounces / 200 g (½ of a 14-ounce package) firm tofu (두부 dubu), cut into medium dice

1 green or red Korean chile pepper or jalapeño pepper, cut into thin slices (optional, for spicy heat)

1 scallion, thinly sliced, for garnish

Rice, for serving

1. To make the stew base: Combine the water, kelp, shiitakes, soybean paste, and garlic in a medium pot and bring to a boil over medium heat.

2. Add the squash, onion, button mushrooms, tofu, and chile pepper, if using, and bring to a boil over high heat. Reduce the heat to medium-low and simmer until all ingredients are cooked thoroughly, about 10 minutes. Taste and add more soybean paste to your preference.

3. Sprinkle with the scallion and serve hot with rice.

SIMPLE KIMCHI STEW

(김치찌개 Kimchi Jjigae)

Kimchi is a staple Korean dish that is paired with a wide range of dishes. Spicy, fresh kimchi is a fiery salad on its own, but as the fermentation process continues throughout the life of kimchi, its flavor deepens beyond spicy heat and evolves into a complex flavor bomb. Kimchi is great as its uncooked, fermented self, but when it is cooked in countless ways, it is revived as a whole new dish showing a new deep, mellow side. Start cooking with kimchi by making this kimchi stew, which is perfect simply with a bowl of rice. Use the well-fermented vegan kimchi from this book to make it a vegan version, or feel free to use any ripened napa cabbage kimchi.

Makes 4 main servings

1 tablespoon neutral vegetable oil

2 cups / 500 g vegan kimchi, store-bought or homemade (page 2), cut into bite-size pieces

1 medium onion, diced

1 tablespoon toasted sesame oil

1 medium russet potato, peeled and cut into bite-size pieces

4 to 6 cups / 1 to 1½ liters vegetable stock or water

¼ cup / 60 ml liquid from the kimchi jar

1 teaspoon Korean fermented soybean paste (된장 doenjang)

1 (14-ounce / 400-g) package firm tofu (두부 dubu), cut into bite-size cubes

2 scallions, thinly sliced

Rice, for serving

1. Heat the oil in a medium saucepan over medium heat. Add the kimchi, onion, and sesame oil and sauté until the onion is translucent and the kimchi opaque, about 5 minutes. Mix in the potato pieces and sauté for another minute or so, until the kimchi seasoning starts sticking to the bottom of the pan.

2. Add 4 cups of the stock, the kimchi liquid, and soybean paste and bring to a boil over high heat. Gently add the tofu cubes and bring up to a boil again. Reduce the heat and simmer until the potato is tender, about 5 minutes. Add more stock per your preference, stir to combine, and bring to a boil.

3. Right before serving, sprinkle scallions on top for garnish. Serve with rice.

MAKE AHEAD

Most stews and soups taste better the next day, and kimchi jjigae is no exception. While it can be a quick recipe, you can also make it a couple of hours ahead, except for the scallion garnish at the end. Add the scallions after reheating the stew over medium heat, right before serving.

SPICY RICE CAKE STEW

(떡볶이전골 Tteokbokki Jeongol)

Koreans grow up eating spicy rice cakes from the earliest school days, so this simple street food becomes a comfort food for many grown-up Koreans. The flavor from the street version that everyone recognizes is big, loud, and comforting. Although I use natural ingredients such as shiitakes and cabbage to enhance the savory punch in this hearty stew, it still is a comfort dish of guilty pleasure. If you have access to a Korean market, look for freshly made rice cake sticks that have a better, pillowy-chewy texture.

Makes 4 main servings

4 cups / 700 g rice cake sticks, fresh or from the refrigerated section of a Korean market

8 ounces / 240 g sweet potato starch glass noodles (당면 dangmyeon)

4 dried shiitake mushrooms (표고버섯 pyogo beoseot)

3 cups / 720 ml water

SPICY GOCHUJANG SAUCE

¼ cup / 60 g Korean fermented red pepper paste (고추장 gochujang)

¼ cup / 20 g Korean red pepper flakes

¼ cup / 60 ml soy sauce

2 tablespoons sugar

2 garlic cloves, minced or grated

4 cups / 400 g cabbage, cut into bite-size squares

1 carrot, diagonally sliced

4 scallions, trimmed and cut into 2-inch / 5-cm lengths

2 cups / 480 ml water

Pickled Yellow Radish (page 8), for serving

1. If the rice cake sticks are frozen, soak them in cold water for at least 10 minutes or up to 1 hour. This helps defrost the sticks as well as loosen them up so that they don't stick together during cooking. Skip this step if the rice cake sticks are not frozen.

2. Soak the glass noodles and shiitake mushrooms in the 3 cups / 720 ml water until they are soft enough to handle, about 20 minutes.

3. To make the spicy gochujang sauce: Mix all the ingredients together.

4. Place the cabbage, carrot, and scallions in a large pan. Drain the rice cake sticks and place them on the vegetable bed. Add the gochujang sauce and the 2 cups / 480 ml water. Cover and bring to a boil over medium heat, stirring occasionally with a wooden spoon to make sure the rice cakes don't stick to the bottom.

5. When the mixture comes to a boil, add the glass noodles and softened shiitake mushrooms along with their soaking water. Reduce the heat and simmer until the glass noodles and rice cakes are soft, about 10 minutes. Frozen rice cakes may take longer to soften.

6. Taste and adjust seasoning to your preference. Serve hot with the pickled yellow radish.

VELVETY KABOCHA SQUASH SOUP

(단호박스프 Danhobak Supeu)

This rich, savory-sweet soup evolved from a delicious failure years ago when I tried to make kabocha rice cake for a sweet treat. It turned out too loose to become a rice cake, so I just added water and enjoyed it as a soup. It also tastes much like the traditional Korean pumpkin porridge, but with a smooth, creamy texture. Danhobak, a.k.a. kabocha in the U.S., is my favorite squash to cook with because of its natural, packed sweetness and its small size that can be cooked whole in a pot. Pine nuts are common in traditional Korean royal court cooking, but feel free to try other nuts for variation.

Makes 4 servings

½ cup / 110 g short-grain white rice (a.k.a. sushi rice), rinsed in cold water

1 cup / 240 ml water

1 kabocha squash (단호박 danhobak)

½ cup / 70 g pine nuts, toasted

1 teaspoon kosher salt

1 cup / 240 ml plant-based milk or cow's milk

Toasted pumpkin seeds, for garnish (optional)

1. Soak the rice in the water for 30 minutes. You can prepare this part ahead by soaking the rice up to overnight in the refrigerator.

2. Cook the whole kabocha until soft: 5 to 7 minutes in the microwave or about 20 minutes in boiling water over high heat. Drain and let sit for a few minutes, until cool enough to handle. Cut in half and scoop out and discard seeds. Scoop out 2 cups / 480 g of the flesh. Store the rest of the flesh in a freezer bag in the freezer for another use.

3. In a blender, blend the rice and its soaking water with the squash flesh, pine nuts, and salt to a smooth consistency.

4. Transfer to a medium saucepan and bring to a boil over medium heat, stirring often. The liquid thickens first as big bubbles come up. Cook for about 15 minutes, until it starts to loosen again. Taste to make sure everything is soft.

5. Add the milk and bring to a boil over medium heat, constantly stirring. Feel free to add more milk to loosen the soup consistency to your preference. You can enjoy the soup as is. Or, for a velvety smooth soup, let it cool until warm or room temperature, then blend one more time. Reheat to warm if necessary. Sprinkle with the pumpkin seeds for garnish, if using.

CHILLED CUCUMBER AND SEAWEED SOUP

(오이미역냉국 Oi Miyeok Naeng Guk)

A sip of this tangy, savory broth with crunchy cucumbers makes a good start to a Korean meal on a hot summer day. It's hard to stop at one sip, and you may want to enjoy a whole bowl of it—in which case, make it a complete meal by using it as a base for chilled noodle soup! Even with this simple soup, possibilities are endless: Use the mix of cucumbers and seaweed as directed for a multidimensional savory flavor, or use only cucumbers for a more cooling bite. You can also add a few slices of raw red onion for a hint of spicy heat and that pretty red color.

Makes 4 servings

SOUP BASE

4 cups / 1 liter water

2 tablespoons rice vinegar

2 tablespoons sugar

1 teaspoon kosher salt

1 teaspoon Korean soup soy sauce (국간장 guk ganjang) or regular soy sauce

¼ cup / 5 g dried wakame seaweed (미역 miyeok)

1 cup / 240 ml water

2 Persian cucumbers (a.k.a. mini cucumbers)

1 tablespoon coarse sea salt

2 scallions, thinly sliced

1 tablespoon rice vinegar

1 garlic clove, minced or grated

2 teaspoons grated peeled ginger

1 teaspoon toasted sesame seeds, crushed

½ teaspoon Korean red pepper flakes (optional, for spicy heat)

1. To prepare the soup base: Mix together all the ingredients in a large bowl. Make sure that the sugar and salt are completely dissolved. Refrigerate for at least 30 minutes, or up to overnight.

2. Soak the seaweed in the water until tender, about 20 minutes. Drain and squeeze the seaweed to remove excess water. If the seaweed pieces are big, cut into bite-size pieces.

3. Cut the cucumbers into thin rounds and toss with the sea salt. When the cucumbers start to sweat, about 10 minutes, rinse off the salt with cold water and squeeze out excess water.

4. In a large bowl, toss the seaweed and cucumbers with the scallions, rice vinegar, garlic, ginger, sesame seeds, and red pepper flakes, if using. Let rest in the refrigerator until the flavors settle, 30 minutes to an hour.

5. To serve, pour the soup base into the seasoned seaweed and cucumber and mix.

BUSAN

I am drawn to coastal cities, and this second-largest city in South Korea on the southeastern tip of the peninsula has my heart. Futuristic high-rises, traditional markets, wide beaches, and hilly neighborhoods… It is a city with the endless lure of contrasts.

VEGETARIAN DISHES FROM MY KOREAN HOME

Noodles and Rice

A Korean meal is considered complete only if it is accompanied by or ends with a rice or noodle dish. The recipes here can be stand-alone, one-bowl dishes or a part of your festive Korean meal.

ONE-PAN GLASS NOODLES WITH VEGETABLES

(잡채 Japchae)

This popular main dish features the bouncy, soft-chewy Korean glass noodles called dangmyeon (당면), which are made from sweet potato starch. In the traditional japchae, each vegetable is stir-fried separately and mixed together right before serving so that the flavor of each ingredient is preserved to the end. Out of laziness but still full of cravings for japchae, I came up with this simpler one-pan version and have been happily making it for years. It is still flavorful but uses less oil—and you will have fewer dishes to wash.

Makes 4 main servings

4 cups / 1 liter lukewarm water

¼ cup / 60 ml soy sauce

4 garlic cloves, minced or grated

1 teaspoon grated peeled ginger

8 ounces / 240 g glass noodles
(당면 dangmyeon)

4 dried shiitake mushrooms
(표고버섯 pyogo beoseot)

2 teaspoons neutral vegetable oil

1 medium onion, thinly sliced

1 medium carrot, peeled and
cut into matchsticks

1 red bell pepper, seeded and
cut into matchsticks

Pinch kosher salt

2 packed cups / 60 g spinach
(시금치 sigeumchi) leaves

Pinch ground black pepper

1 to 2 tablespoons toasted sesame oil

2 teaspoons toasted
sesame seeds, for garnish

1. Mix the water, soy sauce, garlic, and ginger in a medium bowl or rectangular pan. Add the glass noodles and shiitakes and soak in the seasoned water until soft, about 30 minutes. Squeeze out excess water from the mushrooms, cut into thin slices, and return to the seasoned water.

2. Heat a large skillet over medium heat. Drizzle in the oil, then add the onion, carrot, bell pepper, and salt. Sauté over medium heat until the onion turns translucent, about 3 minutes.

3. Add the glass noodles, mushroom slices, and 1½ cups of their seasoned water. Turn the heat to high and cook until the noodles are tender but still with a chewy bite, about 10 minutes; stir occasionally to cook the noodles evenly. The liquid should be mostly incorporated by this point; if the noodles look too dry, add some of the remaining seasoned water and continue cooking the noodles.

4. Add the spinach to the skillet and mix gently to combine. Steam from the dish should be enough to wilt the spinach in a couple of minutes. Add a pinch of ground black pepper and remove from the heat.

5. Taste and adjust seasoning if necessary. Right before serving, drizzle in sesame oil to taste. Sprinkle sesame seeds for garnish and serve immediately.

VEGETARIAN DISHES FROM MY KOREAN HOME

SPICY NOODLE SALAD

(비빔국수 Bibim Guksu)

On a hot summer day, this is my go-to salad, with brightly colored, crunchy vegetables and cooling buckwheat noodles in each bite. The spicy, tangy sauce that makes the whole dish delightful has a deep heat from gochujang that is balanced by a refreshing mix of vinegar and honey. I like substituting a portion of vinegar with fresh lemon juice for brighter acidity, but feel free to use 4 tablespoons rice vinegar and omit the lemon juice. Bookmark the sauce and try it on other salads and even as a bibimbap sauce. For this noodle salad, grab any vegetables of your choice in the season's bounty—just make sure to cut them into matchsticks so that it's easy to scoop up the variety in one chopstick bite.

Makes 4 servings

SPICY TANGY GOCHUJANG SAUCE

¼ cup / 60 g Korean fermented red pepper paste (고추장 gochujang)

2 tablespoons rice vinegar

2 tablespoons fresh lemon juice

2 tablespoons soy sauce

2 tablespoons honey

4 bundles (14 ounces / 400 g) dried buckwheat soba noodles (메밀면 maemil myeon)

2 tablespoons toasted sesame oil

1 cup / 90 g sliced cabbage

1 small carrot, cut into matchsticks

1 English cucumber, cut into matchsticks

1 red bell pepper (or a mix of different colored bell peppers), seeded and cut into matchsticks

2 to 3 perilla leaves (깻잎 ggaet nip) or mint leaves from 1 sprig, slivered (optional)

1. To make the spicy tangy gochujang sauce: Mix all the ingredients together in a small bowl.

2. Cook the buckwheat noodles per package directions. Rinse in cold water until the noodles are completely cooled. Drain, transfer to a large bowl, and mix in the sesame oil.

3. Add half of the sauce to the buckwheat noodles and mix to coat. Add the vegetables, including perilla leaves, if using, and the remaining sauce and mix completely with the noodles. Serve chilled.

KIMCHI FRIED RICE

(김치볶음밥 Kimchi Bokkeum Bap)

Kimchi is easily adaptable as an ingredient for other dishes. Its deep, complex fermented goodness comes alive in a new way without losing its identity. Since kimchi is already heavily seasoned with added layers of flavors from fermentation, you need only a handful of ingredients if you cook with good kimchi—aged, tart, or even a bit too sour to be eaten as it is. To make sure this simple vegan version is lip-smacking delicious, I start by releasing scallion flavors in oil for the base of the fried rice. It's a new trick I learned from watching *Mr. Baek, the Homemade Food Master,* the hit cooking show in Korea.

Makes 2 to 3 servings

3 tablespoons neutral vegetable oil

5 scallions, thinly sliced

1 cup / 250 g vegan kimchi, store-bought or homemade (page 2), chopped

1 tablespoon Korean red pepper flakes

Pinch ground black pepper

2 to 2½ cups / 320 to 400 g cooked rice

½ to 1 teaspoon soy sauce, if needed

1 tablespoon toasted sesame oil

½ teaspoon toasted sesame seeds, for garnish (optional)

1 sheet toasted nori seaweed (김 gim), for garnish (optional)

2 to 3 eggs, cooked sunny-side up (optional)

1. Drizzle the oil into a medium skillet and add the scallions. Cook over medium-low heat, stirring occasionally with a wooden spoon, until the scallions are tender, about 5 minutes.

2. Add the kimchi, red pepper flakes, and ground black pepper and sauté until the kimchi pieces turn opaque and the red pepper flakes start sticking to the bottom of the pan.

3. Turn off the heat. Thoroughly mix 2 cups of the rice into the kimchi until there are no white spots. Taste, and if it's too salty, add more rice. If it's too bland, adjust seasoning with the soy sauce.

4. Drizzle in the toasted sesame oil and mix thoroughly. If you like, sprinkle with toasted sesame seeds for garnish. Crumble the nori seaweed all over and top with the fried eggs, if you like. Serve hot.

RICE WITH ASSORTED VEGETABLES

(비빔밥 Bibimbap)

In the picture of bibimbap that many people now recognize, a fried egg is surrounded by pretty, colorful vegetables in a large bowl. Each vegetable is prepared and carefully arranged on a bed of rice, and it takes a lot of effort. But at home, bibimbap is a quick meal or a late-night snack Koreans put together on the fly. With a repertoire of banchan on hand at all times—fermented, preserved, dry, and fresh dishes, some leftover rice (there is always some leftover rice in the rice cooker or in the refrigerator), and the basic pantry items of gochujang, sesame oil, sesame seeds, and rice vinegar, we make bibimbap with what we have. Sometimes we may skip the arranging of the vegetables by color and get right to mixing them all together. There is no wrong answer to a home version of bibimbap. Everyone has his or her own home bibimbap.

Makes 4 main servings

BIBIMBAP SAUCE

¼ cup / 60 g Korean fermented red pepper paste (고추장 gochujang)

2 tablespoons toasted sesame oil

1 tablespoon rice vinegar

1 teaspoon honey or agave syrup

1 teaspoon toasted sesame seeds

1 garlic clove, minced or grated

8 dried shiitake mushrooms (표고버섯 pyogo beoseot)

½ cup / 120 ml warm water

1½ teaspoons neutral vegetable oil

Kosher salt

Ground black pepper

1 carrot

1 yellow zucchini

2 cups / 480 ml water

1. To make the bibimbap sauce: Whisk the ingredients together to combine in a medium bowl.

2. Soak the shiitakes in the warm water until soft, about 20 minutes. Squeeze to remove excess water and cut into thin slices. Heat a medium skillet over medium heat. Drizzle in ½ teaspoon of the oil and sauté the mushroom slices until soft. Add a pinch of salt and pepper and stir. Transfer the mushrooms to a plate.

3. Peel the carrot and cut off the top. Cut into matchsticks, or keep peeling with a vegetable peeler to make long, thin carrot ribbons, then gather the ribbons and cut them in half. Sauté the carrot with ½ teaspoon of the remaining oil. Sprinkle with a pinch of salt and pepper and stir to mix. Transfer to a plate.

4. Cut off the top of the zucchini, then cut in half lengthwise. Cut into thin half-moons. Dissolve 1 tablespoon salt in the 2 cups water and soak the zucchini slices until the middle parts start turning translucent, about 10 minutes. Drain and rinse off the salt. Sauté the zucchini in the remaining ½ teaspoon oil with a pinch of salt and pepper until the middles turn translucent, about 5 minutes. Transfer to a plate.

CONT. NEXT PAGE...

RICE WITH ASSORTED VEGETABLES, CONT.

2 cups cooked brown rice
(short- or medium-grain sticky rice)

4 eggs, cooked
sunny-side up (optional)

Spinach in Sesame Seasoning (page 32)

1 tablespoon toasted sesame oil

1 teaspoon toasted sesame seeds, crushed

5. To serve, divide the rice among 4 serving bowls and top each with a sunny-side up egg, if using. Arrange the sautéed vegetables and the spinach around the eggs. Top each serving with a dollop of sauce, a drizzle of sesame oil, and a sprinkle of sesame seeds. Alternatively, set up a bibimbap station by laying out the vegetables separately so the guests can pick and choose. In both cases, place more sauce and sesame oil on the table for the guests to help themselves.

VEGETARIAN DISHES FROM MY KOREAN HOME

Desserts

Traditional Korean desserts rely on natural ingredients to infuse their own subtle sweet note in the dish. This short list of sweets spans from traditional to modern, all of them with the ease of making in mind.

STEAMED PEARS
WITH HONEY AND GINGER

(배찜 Bae Jjim)

In Korea, steamed pears are said to be the best homeopathic remedy for the common cold in the wintertime. But even without any cold symptoms, the sweet treat is a heartwarming dessert, especially if you present it in whole-pear form. Asian pears are eaten when they are firm and juicy, just like apples. If you can't find Asian pears in Korean or Asian markets, substitute ripe Bosc pears.

Makes 4 servings

4 small, firm Asian pears, a.k.a. apple pears (배 bae)

2 tablespoons peeled and grated ginger

2 tablespoons honey or agave syrup

1 to 2 cinnamon sticks, broken into 4 sticks

1. Wash the pears thoroughly.

2. Cut off about ½ inch / 1 cm of the top of each pear and set aside. Using a melon baller or a teaspoon, scoop out the inside, being careful not to puncture through the bottom. Discard the seeds from the scooped-out flesh.

3. Mix the scooped pear flesh with the ginger, then use the mixture to fill the pear cavities. Drizzle the honey over the filling and put the tops back on as lids. Secure the tops with the pieces of cinnamon stick. Place each pear in a heat-resistant bowl.

4. Set up a steamer insert in a big pot and add water to the pot to just below the insert. Bring the water to a boil over high heat, then place the bowls with the pears in the steamer insert. Cover and steam over medium heat until the pears are completely soft, 40 minutes to 1 hour. Uncover and check once in a while to make sure there is enough water in the pot for steaming and add more water as necessary. Serve warm.

NO-STEAMER VERSION

You can also cut the pears into bite-size pieces, mix them with the rest of the ingredients, and place in a medium pot with enough water to barely cover the pears. Cover and simmer over low heat until the pears are soft, about 40 minutes. Check once in a while and add more water as necessary, just enough to keep the bottom of the pot covered in liquid at all times.

RICE BARS

(오븐떡 Obeun Tteok)

This treat made with sweet rice flour is the best of both worlds with a crispy outside—like crackly cookies—and a gooey and soft-chewy inside—like traditional rice cakes. I use a baking sheet and spread the batter thinly, like chocolate bark, to maximize the crispy surfaces. But feel free to use a deeper, smaller bread pan or brownie pan (and bake about 10 minutes longer) to maximize the soft, pillowy rice cake texture. Chickpeas, dried cranberries, and pecans are my favorite combination of add-ins. But be creative with your own selection of nuts, seeds, dried fruits, and even cooked beans, which are common in both savory and sweet Korean dishes.

Makes about 24 bars

1 tablespoon neutral vegetable oil, for greasing the parchment paper

2 cups / 300 g sweet rice flour (a.k.a. glutinous rice flour; Mochiko or Bob's Red Mill brand)

¼ cup / 40 g sugar

1 teaspoon baking powder

½ teaspoon kosher salt

1 egg

1½ cups / 355 ml plant-based milk, cow's milk, or water

1 (15.5-ounce / 440-g) can chickpeas (a.k.a. garbanzo beans), drained

½ cup / 65 g dried cranberries, roughly chopped

½ cup / 60 g toasted pecans, roughly chopped

1. Preheat the oven to 350°F / 160°C. Line a baking sheet with parchment paper and grease the parchment with the oil. Set aside.

2. Mix together the flour, sugar, baking powder, and salt in a large bowl. In a separate bowl, whisk the egg, then mix in the milk. Add the wet ingredients to the dry ingredients and combine completely with a wooden spoon.

3. Add the chickpeas, cranberries, and pecans to the batter and fold to combine thoroughly.

4. Pour the batter onto the parchment-lined baking sheet and spread in a thin, even layer. Bake until the top is crackly and golden brown, 50 minutes to 1 hour.

5. Cool on a rack to room temperature. Remove the parchment paper and cut the rice cake into small bars. Serve warm.

6. Any leftovers can be stored in the freezer for up to 2 weeks. Reheat a few pieces at a time in a microwave for 30 seconds. Or, to revive the crispy outer texture, reheat on a baking sheet in a 350°F / 160°C oven for about 10 minutes, just until warm.

VEGETARIAN DISHES FROM MY KOREAN HOME

SWEET CINNAMON-GINGER TEA

(수정과 Sujeonggwa)

This is one of the easiest Korean sweet drinks you can make! The trick to releasing the ginger flavor is to simmer the tea for an hour or longer. Serve as a refreshing pick-me-up with a mild sweetness, or make it with more sugar for a concentrated cocktail mix. Anyone up for soju and sujeonggwa on the rocks?

Makes 7 cups / 1.7 liters, 7 to 8 servings

1 (3-inch / 7.5-cm) cinnamon stick

1 (2-inch / 5-cm) piece ginger, peeled and cut into thin slices

8 cups / 2 liters water

¼ to ½ cup / 40 to 80 g brown sugar

1 tablespoon toasted pine nuts, for garnish (optional)

1. Clean the cinnamon stick by breaking it into a few pieces and washing under running water.

2. In a large saucepan, combine the cinnamon pieces, ginger, and water and bring to a boil over high heat. Reduce the heat to low and simmer for 1 hour or longer, until the cinnamon pieces unfold.

3. Remove the cinnamon and discard. Add ¼ cup brown sugar to the tea and stir to dissolve. When the tea has cooled to room temperature, taste and add more sugar to your preference.

4. Serve hot or cold. Float a few pine nuts for garnish, if you like. Store in the refrigerator for up to 3 days.

SEOUL

Seoul is the backdrop of my childhood memories, painted in a warm antique filter in my heart. Every time I return home, I still find new juxtaposition of old and new in hidden corners of this vast, fast-paced, and ever-changing city.

VEGETARIAN DISHES FROM MY KOREAN HOME

NEW YORK CITY

I have been calling New York City my home since 2005. NYC gave me the courage and resources to plunge into a completely different path. I have learned the discipline of cooking, rediscovered my appreciation for Korean food, and along the way, I've cried and laughed like I had never before.

I look forward to expanding my knowledge about Korean culinary culture whenever I can and to sharing my passion in different capacities. Clockwise, from top left: (1) Learning to make Korean temple cuisine at the temple cuisine restaurant Baloo Gongyang, Seoul; (2) Leading a conversation with Food Director Soo Jin Kim at the Korea Society, NYC; (3) Teaching cooking workshops with Culinary Corps chef volunteers at Camp Sunshine, which offers retreats for children fighting cancer; and (4) Hosting a Korean New Year cooking class through my Banchan Story program.